UNconditional?

SMALL GROUP DISCUSSION GUIDE

Brian Zahnd

Charisma
HOUSE
A STRANG COMPANY

Most STRANG COMMUNICATIONS BOOK GROUP products are available at special quantity discounts for bulk purchase for sales promotions, premiums, fund-raising, and educational needs. For details, write Strang Communications Book Group, 600 Rinehart Road, Lake Mary, Florida 32746, or telephone (407) 333-0600.

UNCONDITIONAL? SMALL GROUP DISCUSSION GUIDE by Brian Zahnd
Published by Ministry Today Books
A Strang Company
600 Rinehart Road
Lake Mary, Florida 32746
www.strangbookgroup.com

Unless otherwise noted, all Scripture quotations are from the Holy Bible, English Standard Version. Copyright © 2001 by Crossway Bibles, a division of Good News Publishers. Used by permission.

Scripture quotations marked NIV are from the Holy Bible, New International Version. Copyright © 1973, 1978, 1984, International Bible Society. Used by permission.

Scripture quotations marked NKJV are from the New King James Version of the Bible. Copyright © 1979, 1980, 1982 by Thomas Nelson, Inc., publishers. Used by permission.

Scripture quotations marked NLT are from the Holy Bible, New Living Translation, copyright © 1996. Used by permission of Tyndale House Publishers, Inc., Wheaton, IL 60189. All rights reserved.

Scripture quotations marked THE MESSAGE are from *The Message: The Bible in Contemporary English*, copyright © 1993, 1994, 1995, 1996, 2000, 2001, 2002. Used by permission of NavPress Publishing Group.

Cover design by Justin Evans
Design Director: Bill Johnson

Visit the author's website at www.brianzahnd.com.

Library of Congress Control Number: 2010938525
International Standard Book Number: 978-1-61638-351-0
E-book ISBN: 978-1-61638-417-3
11 12 13 14 15 — 9 8 7 6 5 4 3 2 1
Printed in the United States of America

CONTENTS

INTRODUCTION

IT SHOULD BE obvious that forgiveness lies at the heart of the Christian faith, for at its most crucial moments the gracious melody of forgiveness is heard as the recurring theme of Christianity. Whether we look to the Lord's Prayer or Jesus's death upon the cross or his resurrection or the great creeds of the church, we are never far from the theme of forgiveness—for if Christianity isn't about forgiveness, it's about nothing at all.

Whatever else may be said about Christian people, it must be said of us that we are a people who believe in the forgiveness of sins—we believe in the forgiveness of sins as surely as we believe in the death and resurrection of Jesus Christ. Most of us enter the Christian faith at least somewhat motivated, if not primarily motivated, to find forgiveness for our own sins. As we grow in the Christian faith, it is vital we become aware that we are called to be those who extend forgiveness to others, thus making the world a more forgiving place. If we enter the Christian faith to find forgiveness, we must continue in the faith to become forgiving people, because to be an authentic follower of Christ we must embrace the centrality of forgiveness.

Yet many people today—even many believers—struggle with issues of forgiveness. How viable is forgiveness in the real world of murder, rape, child abuse, genocide, and other horrible atrocities? Is there a limit for forgiveness? Are there some crimes that go beyond the capacity of forgiveness? Are there some sins so heinous that to forgive them would itself be an immoral act? Is forgiveness always possible? Or even always right? These are not theoretical questions; these are real questions that are forced upon us in a world where evil is so often beyond the pale.

For example, can the genocide of the Holocaust be forgiven? If you have read all of *Unconditional?*, you know that Simon Wiesenthal could not forgive the atrocities he witnessed in the Nazi concentration camp where he was imprisoned during World War II. Like Wiesenthal, Corrie ten Boom was also imprisoned in a Nazi concentration camp, but she was able to extend forgiveness to the German guard responsible for hundreds of Jewish deaths—including the deaths of her own parents and sister.

I am fully convinced that to deny the possibility of forgiveness is to deny the very heart of the Christian gospel. Christian forgiveness is not a cheap denial of the reality of evil or the trite sloganeering of "forgive and forget." That may suffice for minor personal affronts, but it is hollow and even insulting when applied to crimes like murder, rape, and genocide. No, Christian forgiveness is not cheap. Rather it is costly because it flows from the cross—the place where injustice and forgiveness meet in a violent collision. Christian forgiveness does not call us to forget. Christian forgiveness allows us to remember but calls us to end the cycle of revenge.

For the committed Christ follower, the question of forgiveness is not a question of whether forgiveness is possible, but a question of how we can find the grace to offer forgiveness. We may discover that we offer forgiveness to transgressors and offenders the same way that Jesus did—amidst great suffering. In our feelings-oriented culture, it's easy to equate forgiveness with having certain feelings. Forgiveness is not a feeling. Forgiveness is a choice to end the cycle of revenge and leave justice in the hands of God.

This small group discussion guide will provide you with an opportunity to consider if you have made—or will make—the choice to be forgiving. Before each group session you will have the time to read the chapter from *Unconditional?* that is the foundation for that week's study. I trust you will also contribute fully with your group, honestly sharing your heart as your group is challenged with the question of forgiveness. And there will be reflective questions for you to answer and action steps that you can take after each session that I hope will bring you—through the power of God's gift of grace—to the point of determining to make the choice to live your life in forgiveness.

Each week's study is broken into five sections. The READ section will tell you what chapter from *Unconditional?* will be used as the foundation focus for that session. It will also help you to summarize the main points in that chapter. The REFLECT section will draw you into the Word of God to prepare you with the biblical principles for that session. The DISCUSS section provides the questions you will discuss and explore together as a group. The WRAP UP section helps to make this study specifically applicable to your own life as you think about the group's discussions. Finally, each session ends with a LIVING WORD from the Bible that you can memorize and use to grow spiritually each week.

Remember to approach each session of this study with an open heart and mind. Be ready to share your own struggles with forgiveness, and listen with acceptance as others share their stories. Grow together through this study, and learn to experience the peace of God that is possible only through the power of forgiveness.

READING SCHEDULE FOR *UNCONDITIONAL?*

Session 1: Read chapter 2, "The Possibility of Forgiveness"

Session 2: Read chapter 3, "The Imitation of Christ"

Session 3: Read chapter 4, "No Future Without Forgiveness"

Session 4: Read chapter 6, "Forgiveness and Justice"

Session 5: Read chapter 8, "The Golden Rule and the Narrow Gate"

Session 6: Read chapter 10, "The Prince of Peace"

{ Even if we don't want to think
about forgiveness on a global
or cosmic scale, preferring
to keep the possibilities of
forgiveness to a personal level,
there's no getting around the
fact that Jesus challenges our
limited ideas regarding the
extent of forgiveness. }

THE POSSIBILITY OF FORGIVENESS

READ

Read chapter 2 from *Unconditional?* before you meet with the group this week.

THE ISSUE ISN'T whether forgiveness is a good thing—most people believe it is. The issue is how far we should go in forgiving. I suppose no one lives without occasionally offering some measure of forgiveness to those around him. To live without ever extending forgiveness, for at least minor infringements, would seem to make it nearly impossible to get on in life with any kind of normalcy. The burden of holding on to every perceived slight or imagined infraction would make life unbearable. Even the most coldhearted and embittered soul may forgive someone for stepping on his or her toes. To maintain even the most cursory level of social interaction, there must be a willingness to overlook the occasional trifling affront. The real question is: To what extent are we expected to forgive? How far shall we go in forgiving? How much can be forgiven? How often can we forgive? What are the possibilities of forgiveness?

REFLECT

Take time to consider each of the questions in this section before you meet with your group, and be prepared to share your answers.

Peter was questioning Jesus about the extent of forgiveness when he asked Jesus, "How often will my brother sin against me, and I forgive him?" (Matt. 18:21). And before Jesus has an opportunity to answer, Peter puts forth his own idea regarding the extent of forgiveness—"As many as seven times?" I have little doubt that Peter was feeling quite generous and was rather pleased by what he perceived as a magnanimous offer of forgiveness—forgiveness times seven! Seven is a divine number, so surely forgiving seven times must be considered a divine act and would fill up the possibility of forgiveness. Surely one would not be expected to go beyond forgiving an offender seven times. But we should know by now that our presumption about what Jesus will say and our assumption that he will endorse our opinion are almost always misplaced. Jesus is the Christ of perpetual surprise, and those who walk with Jesus soon discover this. Peter certainly did. Can you imagine Peter's astonishment when Jesus said, "I do not say to you seven times, but seventy times seven" (v. 22). *Seventy times seven!* Peter didn't see that coming.

[Q]

Can you name a situation in your own life that might require you offering forgiveness to someone seventy times seven?

2

When Jesus says repeatedly in the Sermon on the Mount, "You have heard it said…but I say to you," he was daring to challenge the Torah (the Jewish Scriptures). Moses called for a reciprocal response to injustice and injury— "life for life, eye for eye, tooth for tooth, hand for hand, foot for foot, burn for burn, wound for wound, stripe for stripe" (Exod. 21:23–25). But Jesus calls for the counterintuitive response of turning the other cheek. Instead of a reciprocal response, Jesus calls for radical forgiveness. Turning the other cheek, though perhaps heard as a cliché today, is still a very difficult demand that forces us to push the boundaries on the possibilities of forgiveness. But the Christ follower does not have the option to choose Moses's reciprocal response over Jesus's radical forgiveness. Jesus calls his disciples to a different way, a better way, a higher way, and ultimately, a necessary way.

[Q]

Meditate on the fact that Jesus called his disciples to a different way, a better way, a higher way, and ultimately, a necessary way. Give an example of a situation today that would force a choice between an *eye for an eye* choice or a *better way* choice. How would you choose in that situation?

After telling the story of Corrie ten Boom in chapter 2, the author writes this: "Corrie ten Boom faced the question of forgiveness in stark reality. She had suffered in a Nazi death camp. She had lost family members in the Holocaust. She had experienced firsthand the cruelty of Nazi prison guards. And she was asked to forgive. She was not asked about the *possibility* of forgiveness; she was asked to *actually* forgive a Nazi who had treated her with callous cruelty and contributed to the death of her sister. And the saintly Corrie ten Boom makes two points quite clear. First, it was not easy to offer forgiveness to a Nazi tormenter, and second, as a Christian she had no choice but to do so. But she also makes the important point that forgiveness is not an emotion; it is an act of the will. In a mechanical act of the will to obey Jesus and offer forgiveness, Corrie ten Boom discovered that the love of God through the Holy Spirit is released, thus making forgiveness genuine and transformative. This is Christianity in its essence. This is Christianity at its finest."

[Q]

Brian Zahnd writes that "forgiveness is not an emotion; it is an act of the will." When have you found it necessary to forgive someone *as an act of your will*? How did you feel after choosing to forgive?

Write a brief sentence about how each of the following verses has been true (or not true) in your experience.

Psalm 85:2: "You forgave the iniquity of your people; you covered all their sin. Selah."

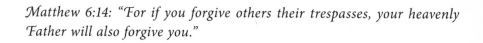

Matthew 6:14: "*For if you forgive others their trespasses, your heavenly Father will also forgive you.*"

Luke 17:3: "*Pay attention to yourselves! If your brother sins, rebuke him, and if he repents, forgive him.*"

James 5:15: "*And the prayer of faith will save the one who is sick, and the Lord will raise him up. And if he has committed sins, he will be forgiven.*"

DISCUSS

When your small group is meeting to discuss this chapter, focus on discussing the following questions or statements.

Even if we don't want to think about forgiveness on a global or cosmic scale, preferring to keep our consideration regarding the possibilities of forgiveness to a personal level, there's no getting around the fact that Jesus challenges our limited ideas regarding the extent of forgiveness. Not seven times. Seventy times seven!

[Q]

When Jesus says to Peter (and to us) not seven times, but seventy times seven, what is he saying? Isn't he saying that we must always find a way to forgive? Isn't he suggesting that the possibilities of forgiveness are endless? That to be sinned against is to be called to forgive?

It is by the Holy Spirit that the possibilities of forgiveness are expanded to the infinite. We are not called to infinitely forgive on our own. This would be to ask the impossible. Rather we are called to make the difficult choice to forgive as an act of obedience to Jesus Christ and then to become a channel through which the Holy Spirit brings the love of God into a deeply broken and alienated world. Christian forgiveness that extends seventy times seven is not an act of the lone individual but an act in concert with the entire Trinity. Christian forgiveness that pushes the possibilities into the infinite involves the love of God, the resurrection of Jesus Christ, and the baptism in the Holy Spirit. In a sacred dance with the Trinity, we become agents of the reconciliation whereby God is bringing healing into a world crippled by the seemingly unforgivable.

[Q]

When, in your experience, has the Holy Spirit enabled you to make the difficult choice to forgive?

Not only does forgiveness open new possibilities for the future, but forgiveness also gives us a new perspective on the past. In some mysterious way that we may not be able to fully comprehend, forgiveness seems to have the capacity to redeem the past. What would otherwise poison us now has a redemptive quality in our life. This too is part of the possibility of forgiveness. Forgiveness seems to have the capacity to alter suffering from something that is purely destructive to something that has profound redemptive qualities.

[Q]

Share an experience from your life when forgiveness opened the door to new possibilities for you *and* gave you a new perspective on the past.

Chapter 2 tells the story of Tyrese, a man who came from a heritage deeply shaped by America's two greatest sins—the atrocity of African slavery and the systematic destruction of Native Americans. Not only had he experienced forgiveness from Jesus Christ for his own life, but he also understood that he had to extend forgiveness to others. As Tyrese has lived a life of forgiveness, he has seen God reconcile him with his biological parents, give him a wonderful family, and use him to bring saving grace to thousands of people in prison. Because Tyrese embraced the possibility of forgiveness, he has seen God work all things together for good in his life.

[Q]

Can you describe a time when you or someone you know experienced the miracle of reconciliation or restoration in a broken relationship? How did your willingness to forgive begin the process of restoration?

The world of resentment and bitterness is a small, ever-shrinking world. It is a world of ever-diminishing possibilities. It is a world on a trajectory of collapse into the singularity of resentment. Unforgiveness has a devastating way of eliminating new possibilities. Everything remains chained to the past, and the suffered injustice becomes the single informing event in the life of the embittered soul. But the choice to forgive breaks the tyranny of injustice and the bitterness it seeks to create.

[Q]

Can you give an example, either from your life or the life of someone else, when hanging on to resentment, bitterness, and unforgiveness eliminated some new and positive possibility from taking place?

Nikolai Velimirović was a Serbian Orthodox bishop who, during World War II and the German occupation of Yugoslavia, taught against the evils of Nazism to the priests under his charge. He was betrayed by one of the priests, arrested, and sent to the concentration camp at Dachau. It was in Dachau that Nikolai Velimirović learned to pray for his enemy persecutors and, most of all, for the man who had betrayed him. As a prisoner in Dachau, Velimirović composed a prayer known as "Prayer Regarding Critics and Enemies." You can read that prayer in chapter 2 of *Unconditional?*

[Q]

Have you ever been stung by the betrayal of someone with whom you were in relationship? Could you—or have you—learned to pray for the person who betrayed you? What are the points that you would have included in your prayer for them?

WRAP UP

During the next week, continue to reflect on God's great gift of forgiveness to you. Use the journal space below to record the thoughts you have about His forgiveness. Take the time to write your own letter to God, thanking Him for His gift of forgiveness. Then write down the names of people to whom you have given the gift of your forgiveness. How did it make you feel? How did it make them feel? How has it transformed your relationship with that person?

LIVING WORD

Then Peter came up and said to him, "Lord, how often will my brother sin against me, and I forgive him? As many as seven times?" Jesus said to him, "I do not say to you seven times, but seventy times seven."

—Matthew 18:21-22

PRAYER REQUESTS

NOTES

NOTES

NOTES

{ Jesus didn't come to conquer the world with a sword; he came to save the world with a cross. }

THE IMITATION OF CHRIST

READ

Read chapter 3 from *Unconditional?* before you meet with the group this week.

ON THE NORTHEAST side of Jerusalem's Old City there is a gate leading to the Via Dolorosa known as St. Stephen's Gate. It is so named because it's believed to be near the site where the first Christian martyr, St. Stephen, was stoned to death. Stephen was a deacon who served in the Jerusalem church in the early days following Jesus's resurrection. As a preacher, he was a bold and eloquent witness that Jesus was Israel's Messiah. When Stephen was accused of blasphemy for preaching Jesus as Messiah, he was forcibly taken outside the city walls to be executed by stoning—the punishment mandated in the Torah for blasphemers. As the stones began to fly, Stephen began to pray a remarkable prayer. Stephen's prayer is a stunning imitation of Christ, who, a few years earlier and not far from where Stephen was being executed, had prayed, "Father, forgive them, for they know not what they do" (Luke 23:34). Stephen's prayer was similar. It was not an imprecatory prayer calling down curses upon his persecutors, but a prayer of forgiveness. Stephen's last words were these: "Lord, do not hold this sin against them" (Acts 7:60). What an impeccable imitation of Christ! We find Stephen, with his dying breath, praying for the forgiveness of those who were unjustly putting him to death. Stephen, like Jesus, worked miracles, but Stephen never more fully imitated Christ than in his dying prayer of forgiveness.

REFLECT

Take time to consider each of the questions in this section before you meet with your group, and be prepared to share your answers.

Read the story of Stephen's stoning from Acts 7 this week before your group meets. We will discuss how to imitate Christ this week, and as *Unconditional?* states, Stephen was a bold and eloquent imitator of Christlikeness, both in his life and in his death. Scripture says, "They stoned Stephen as he was calling on God" (Acts 7:59, NKJV). Think about the words that Stephen said in his prayer. Only two short phrases from his prayer are recorded in Scripture. Try to put yourself in Stephen's place, and write down the things that you would have said as those stones were striking you and robbing you of life.

[Q]

What words would you include in your prayer?

Judah Maccabeus was the Hammer of God. Jesus of Nazareth was the Lamb of God. They are competing visions of Messiah. One is an avenging messiah bringing the hammer down on Israel's national enemies. The other is a Suffering Servant laying his life down as a lamb to be slaughtered. One perpetuates the cycle of revenge with his hammer. The other ends the cycle of revenge with his cross. We must choose which vision of Messiah we will embrace. Heaven issues its verdict when it declares, "Worthy is the Lamb" (Rev. 5:12).

[Q]

Brian Zahnd told us that still today you and I must choose whether we see Christ as our avenging Messiah who will *pay back* anyone who wrongs or hurt us, or if we see Christ as the sacrificial Lamb who willingly *gave his life* for the sins of the world. Think back to the times of crisis when you have called out to God for his help. Briefly describe a time when you wanted him to *avenge* or *pay back* someone for what that person did to you. Briefly describe a time when you recognized his sacrifice on the cross and imitated him with your own willingness to suffer without thoughts of revenge.

Avenging Messiah

Sacrificial Lamb

[Q]

When we choose to forgive those who intentionally and maliciously harm us instead of perpetuating the cycle of revenge, we become a living imitation of Jesus Christ. And as we do this, we help flood a world hell-bent on paybacks with a forgiveness that washes away sin. Because our current world is so filled with the desire for revenge, there are times when we react to something with revenge rather than with forgiveness. In each of the examples below, determine what would be a *revenge reaction* and what would be a *forgiveness reaction.*

Being cut off in traffic:

Revenge

Forgiveness

Seeing someone get a promotion that you were hoping to get:

Revenge

Forgiveness

Your husband or wife refuses to listen to your side of a disagreement:

Revenge

Forgiveness

[Q]

Now add two examples of your own.

Example 1:

Example 2:

[Q]

You can become *a* Christian in a moment. But to become Christian is another matter. In our evangelical churches we are very adept at teaching people how to become *a* Christian—how to receive the forgiveness available in Christ. We have not been nearly so adept at teaching people how to become Christian—how to become Christlike in a way that helps flood a world hell-bent on vengeance with the grace of forgiveness. In the spaces below, describe first how you became *a* Christian. Then describe the steps that you are choosing to take right now that are helping you to *become* Christian.

How I became a Christian:

Steps I am taking to become Christian:

DISCUSS

When your small group is meeting to discuss this chapter, focus on discussing the following questions or statements.

Today's world seems to be filled with enormous injustice: the rich get richer while the poor get poorer; millions of children in third world countries are starving while food goes to waste in other countries; and in our own country, CEOs of large corporations are getting enormous bonuses while their employees are losing their jobs. The author stated, "We tend to think that there are only two options: payment or punishment. The perpetrator of injustice must be made to pay, and if they can't pay, then they must be punished. Payment or punishment." But to be the recipient of God's extravagant forgiveness in Christ Jesus places an obligation upon the recipient to become the kind of person who embraces the third option, which is neither payment nor punishment—the option of pardon.

[Q]

Discuss this third option—the option of pardon. Do you know of people today who have embraced this third option or pardon? Describe the circumstances that were pardoned.

[Q]

Should all injustice be pardoned? Why, or why not?

In chapter 3, Rachel Tulloch said, "Justice must be about much more than balancing out the wrongs of the world. It must be about making things *right*, about the kind of restoration that does not reverse the pain, but moves beyond it toward something new."

[Q]

As a group, discuss an event or circumstance that has taken place recently, either in your own life or from the life of someone else, that demonstrates how the option of pardon allowed the individuals involved to move beyond pain into something new.

Forgetting is not the same as forgiving. Amnesia is not the answer to a world stuck in the endless cycle of revenge. This is true for the simple reason that memory is an essential part of forming our identity. There are some things that occur in our lives that, if forgotten, would seriously lessen our authenticity.

If certain events were forgotten entirely, we would quite simply not be fully ourselves. Jesus remembered his crucifixion and could show his wounds—his capacity to forgive did not require that he forget. If Stephen forgot his stoning, if John Paul II forgot he was shot, or if Ingrid Betancourt forgot that she was kidnapped for six and a half years, they would all be less themselves. Their suffering is integral to their identity.

Forgetting is not essential in forgiving because the memory of injustice does not require that we eternally lust for revenge. It is possible in the grace of God for all the pain of injustice to be removed while the scar of memory remains—not as a memory that causes the pain to be relived, but as a memory that forms identity and allows the story to move toward a happy ending even though the middle of the story contains undeniable pain.

[Q]

Have you ever chosen to give forgiveness to someone who wronged you, but you struggled with the memory of that wrong? How has that memory helped to define who you are today? How have you moved beyond that moment of pain to a new place...a new circumstance...a new identity?

Yet this does not mean that we need to *try* to remember every injustice we have suffered. There are some things that legitimately can be forgotten without impinging upon our authenticity. When speaking of suffering injustice, it must be remembered that we are not always entirely innocent. There are many times when the hostility in a relationship that has led to hurtful words and events has sprung from mutual disrespect. Both sides have made their contribution to injustice. In a marriage, we call it a fight. But when forgiveness wins the day and the relationship is healed, it is encouraging to know that there is the very real possibility of both parties moving on together in love even beyond the realm of remembering. For them, memory would serve no redeeming purpose. We don't and can't remember everything. What we remember and what we forget are ways of restructuring our past and thereby forging our identities. To live well, there are things to remember and there are things to forget. A perfect memory does not make a perfect person. Sometimes forgiveness is the art of forgetting. But whether in forgetting or in remembering, forgiveness is always the imitation of Christ.

[Q]

We have all heard the saying, "I may forgive, but I'll never forget!" This is not the kind of remembering that is described in the paragraph above. Take a few minutes as a group to discuss the kinds of things that would have no redeeming purpose for remembering.

[Q]

Now share with one another (if you feel comfortable doing this) what wrongs you have chosen to remember that would be better off forgotten. How has this hindered you from imitating Christlikeness to the one who wronged you? What can you do now to move you closer to exercising the *art of forgiveness* so that you can more closely embody the imitation of Christ in your life?

WRAP UP

In this chapter—and as a group—we have realized that forgiveness can save a soul—and not only the soul of the offender but also the soul of the offended. Forgiving injustice by suffering the loss without retaliation, and thus bringing the possibility of redemption to all involved, is the fullest imitation of Christ available to us. As you apply this understanding to your own life and begin to move toward a new identity—a new life free of revenge—to become a better imitator of Christ, journal your thoughts and actions in the space below.

LIVING WORD

And forgive us our debts, as we also have forgiven our debtors.

—Matthew 6:12

PRAYER REQUESTS

NOTES

NOTES

{ Without forgiveness the Bible
doesn't get past Genesis.
Without forgiveness there really
is no future. }

NO FUTURE WITHOUT FORGIVENESS

READ

Read chapter 4 from *Unconditional?* before you meet with the group this week.

OUR HAPPINESS LIES in hope. If we can approach the future with hope, we can be happy. This is because hope is the prevailing attitude that the pain and disappointments of the past do not have to be endlessly repeated. Hope dares to imagine the future as a legitimate alternative to the vicious repetitions of the past. But the refusal to forgive is a toxic memory that endlessly pulls the painful past into the present. The toxic memory of the unforgiven past poisons the present and contaminates the future.

REFLECT

Take time to consider each of the questions in this section before you meet with your group, and be prepared to share your answers.

We can see the toxic attitude of a future without hope expressed by Solomon in the opening lines of his poem *Ecclesiastes*.

> Vanity of vanities, says the Preacher,
> Vanity of vanities! All is vanity....
> What has been is what will be,
> and what has been done is what will be done,
> and there is nothing new under the sun.
> —ECCLESIASTES 1:2, 9

All is vanity. The past must be repeated. The future holds nothing new. There is no hope. Fortunately, the cynicism of Solomon as a divine revelation of the futility of the life estranged from God is not the final word on the possibilities for the future found in Scripture. The prophets (especially Isaiah), the apostles, and, most importantly, Jesus all offer a radically different vision for the future. They don't speak of vanity, futility, and meaningless repetition, but of purpose, meaning, and the possibility of new beginnings. Yet the prophetic and apostolic vision of a hopeful future is predicated upon our willingness to follow Christ and untangle our lives from the past through the practice of forgiveness. For without the practice of Christlike forgiveness, the cynical poet is right—there is nothing new under the sun. Or as Archbishop Desmond Tutu has said, "There is no future without forgiveness."* Forgiveness is both closing the door on a painful past and opening a new door to look toward a hopeful future. In preparation for your group session this week, read each of the following portions of Scripture and then answer the questions found below.

---

* Desmond Tutu, *No Future Without Forgiveness* (New York: Random House, Inc., 2000).

[Q]

Isaiah 35: Describe how unforgiveness is like the wilderness wasteland and desert described in the opening verses of Isaiah 35.

[Q]

Describe how unforgiveness is like blind eyes, stopped-up ears, and a lameness in walking.

[Q]

Luke 5:17–25—the healing of a paralytic man: In this story, Jesus confronts the Pharisees by demonstrating his power to forgive sins as well as to heal bodies. What do you think Jesus was attempting to get the onlookers to understand when he said, "Why are you reasoning in your hearts? Which is easier, to say, 'Your sins are forgiven you,' or to say, 'Rise up and walk'?"

Luke 7:36–50—a sinful woman is forgiven, These scriptures tell the story of the woman who washed Jesus's feet with her costly perfume and wiped them with her hair. When the Pharisee who had invited him to visit questioned why Jesus would touch a sinner, Jesus responded by teaching him a very important lesson about forgiveness—a lesson each of us should also understand.

[Q]

What is the principle of forgiveness that Jesus taught? Describe what you could do that would demonstrate to Jesus your own great love for his great act of forgiving your sins.

DISCUSS

When your small group is meeting to discuss this chapter, focus on discussing the following questions or statements.

The Old Testament patriarch Joseph understood the necessity of forgiveness in closing the door on a painful past in order to open the door to a promising future. Joseph was a dreamer—the eleventh of twelve brothers. He was also the favorite of his father. The favoritism of his father, along with his dreamy optimism, caused his less favored and less visionary brothers to resent him deeply—a resentment deep enough that they could wish him dead. In the end they did not murder him, but they did something nearly as reprehensible: they sold him into slavery and reported him dead.

For the next thirteen years Joseph lived the life of a slave in Egypt. At times he found favor with his superiors and began to rise from his lowly status. At other times he was maliciously vilified and suffered deep injustice. This went on for thirteen years. And thirteen years of unjust suffering is plenty of time to potentially build up a lot of resentment.

[Q]

The story of Joseph shows how deeply revenge can hurt. Because his brothers were so full of revenge, their hateful treatment toward Joseph locked him into thirteen long years of slavery in Egypt. During those thirteen years, Joseph's brothers were locked in their own prison of bitterness and guilt. Describe a situation today that demonstrates the danger of the cycle of revenge and retaliation.

[Q]

Discuss what your group believes it would take to break out of this cycle.

Regarding the story of Joseph, Brian Zahnd states: "In a conventional tale of rags to riches and the inevitable triumph of the good guy, this is where the story would end and the credits would roll. But Joseph's story does *not* end here. Joseph's story does not end here because the story is not really about Joseph but about the whole family of Israel and their salvation. So the story continues until nine years later when Joseph is reunited with his brothers, who are on the verge of starvation and now completely in Joseph's power. Now the tables are turned. Now Joseph has the opportunity to exact his revenge. Now Joseph can have his brothers sold into slavery as they had sold him into slavery. But Joseph does not do this. Instead Joseph forgives his brothers, provides for their families, and saves the seed of Abraham. Forgiveness had provided Israel with a future."

[Q]

Joseph broke the cycle of revenge by absorbing the injustice of his brothers, forgiving them, and trusting God to right the wrongs. He told his brothers, "Don't be afraid of me. Am I God, that I can punish you? You intended to harm me, but God intended it all for good" (Gen. 50:19–20, NLT). Think back to the situation you discussed as a group earlier. What specific action did the group recommend to break out? What scriptures would support this action?

The way of forgiveness does not forget the past, but through truth and reconciliation it finds a way beyond toxic memory. It is the way of restorative justice. Restorative justice is the kind of justice the prophets talked about. This is the kind of justice Jesus wants to bring to a broken world. This is the kind of justice that can happen when we choose to end the cycle of revenge. This is the kind of justice that can happen when we are more interested in restoration than retaliation.

[Q]

As a group, discuss the concept of *restorative justice,* and then list five modern-day situations where the application of restorative justice could end the cycle of revenge. For each situation you name, discuss and write down at least one way justice could be applied.

[Q]

Look up the following scriptures and read each one. Discuss what each verse tells us about restorative justice. Write down the answers your group gives for each verse.

Deuteronomy 10:18

1 Kings 10:9

Psalm 25:9

Proverbs 13:23

Ecclesiastes 5:8

Isaiah 30:18

Zechariah 7:9

WRAP UP

At the close of chapter 4 in *Unconditional?* the author writes, "So what is your story? Who has been cruel to you? Perhaps bitterly cruel. What injustice have you suffered? How have you been mistreated? Perhaps miserably so. Who has cheated you? Abused you? Mistreated you? Lied to you? Lied *about* you? Maybe it was last week. Maybe it was a lifetime ago. As you remember your suffered injustice, how does it affect the way you view the future? Or let me put it another way: What are you waiting for? Are you waiting to get even? A chance for payback? An opportunity to exact your revenge?"

Take the time in this next week to thoughtfully answer the questions above. Journal your thoughts, and at the end of your journal entries, make a commitment to do whatever is necessary to imitate Christ by extending forgiveness in each of those situations. Journal how you will do that in each instance.

LIVING WORD

And Jesus said, "Father, forgive them, for they know not what they do."

—Luke 23:34

PRAYER REQUESTS

NOTES

NOTES

{

The cross is where justice is
reinterpreted by mercy in
order to be redefined as reconciliation. This alone is what
God calls justice.

}

Session 4

FORGIVENESS AND JUSTICE

READ

Read chapter 6 from *Unconditional?* before you meet with the group this week.

IN COMING TO terms with the call of Christ for his disciples to be practitioners of radical forgiveness, we inevitably run into the thorny question of how forgiveness relates to justice. The psalmist envisions a meeting of mercy and truth, an embrace between justice and peace.

> Mercy and Truth meet;
> Justice and Peace kiss.
> —PSALM 85:10, AUTHOR'S TRANSLATION

But in what way? How can mercy and truth meet? How can justice and peace kiss? Is there a way in which the mercy of forgiveness can kiss the truth of justice and it not be a Judas kiss of betrayal? In forgiving, are we just kissing justice good-bye? If we forgive the offender for his or her transgression and let that person *just get away with it*, hasn't justice been betrayed? So we are faced with the troubling question of whether forgiveness and justice are at loggerheads. Do we have to choose one or the other—justice or forgiveness? Are there times when forgiveness and justice are mutually exclusive?

REFLECT

Take time to consider each of the questions in this section before you meet with your group, and be prepared to share your answers.

What do we mean by justice? In the context of our own experience with what we deem to be unfair treatment, the use of the word *justice* probably has something to do with protection or punishment or recompense, or some combination of the three. So when we see ourselves as a victim seeking justice, we generally mean we are seeking *protection* from those who are harming us or would harm us; or we are seeking the *punishment* of those who have harmed us; or we are seeking *recompense* for what we have lost through the unjust actions of others. Of course this is what our legal and criminal justice systems attempt to deliver.

[Q]

Before your group meets and begins to discuss how justice relates to forgiveness, reflect on what you believe to be the definition of justice. Write your definition in the space below.

Brian Zahnd writes, "Justice is not always black and white. Sometimes it's barely discernable. Who is right and who is wrong can be enormously complicated. And when we are involved in a dispute, it would serve us well to remember that our perspective may be limited. Miroslav Volf astutely reminds us, 'When we are looking at each other through the sights of our guns we see only the rightness of our own cause. We think more about how to enlarge our power than to enlarge our thinking.'* Trying to win an argument (much less a war!) isn't usually a very good way of arriving at the truth. Truth is too often sacrificed for the sake of the argument. When we have a stake in the matter, we have a natural tendency to oversimplify what constitutes justice, and often *justice* is little more than *me getting my way.*"

[Q]

Think about the times in your own life when you have been wronged and wanted justice. Were you thinking about who was right and who was wrong in that situation? Were you hoping to win the argument or to be exonerated in the matter? Briefly describe one of these times, and then write down what you believed would *give you justice* in the matter.

The author tells us that, "For those who believe in a God who is personally committed to the cause of justice, forgiveness is an act of *faith*, not weakness. The choice to forgive is not an exoneration of the criminal; it is a choice to end the cycle of revenge and leave the matter of justice in the hands of God." Then he illustrates by introducing us to the *imprecatory psalms*—the *cursing* psalms. These are the angry psalms that plead for God to do justice by inflicting his wrath upon the wicked. The important point he makes is this: *rage against injustice belongs before God.* Instead of holding rage against injustice in our heart, where it is allowed to fester and corrupt, we place our rage against injustice before the throne of God, recognizing that God and God alone is capable of judging the world in righteousness.

---

* Miroslav Volf, *Exclusion and Embrace* (Nashville, TN: Abingdon Press, 1996), 215.

[Q]

What are some overt examples of deep injustice in our world today? How have those involved demonstrated anger and rage against the injustice?

DISCUSS

When your small group is meeting to discuss this chapter, focus on discussing the following questions or statements.

In chapter 6 we learned that God seems to have a predisposition to show a certain kind of partiality to the poor, the widow, the orphan, and the alien. Zahnd writes, "Though it may offend our modern democratic penchant for radical egalitarianism, the witness of Scripture is clear that God is committed to upholding the cause of the weak and the poor in a way that he is not committed to upholding the cause of the strong and rich."

[Q]

As a group, discuss each of the following scriptures, stating what the verse says about God's commitment to the weaker members of society.

Luke 14:13

Exodus 23:11

Leviticus 25:35

Psalm 68:4–6

Malachi 3:5

James 1:27

John 14:18

Isaiah 40:29

2 Corinthians 12:9

In its most basic form, forgiveness is the choice to resist responding to evil with evil, to resist responding to hate with hate, to resist responding to violence with violence, to resist responding to malice with malice. This is the basic requirement of forgiveness. But that alone does not achieve the final goal of justice, which is reconciliation. For reconciliation to occur, there must be repentance on the part of the offender. Forgiveness can happen unilaterally, but reconciliation requires the participation of both parties.

[Q]

Describe times when each of your group members might have suffered an injustice, extended forgiveness to the one who wronged him or her, and then experienced the joy of being reconciled to that person in the bond of friendship.

We are all acutely aware that right now there are escalating conflicts between the countries in the Middle East, particularly between Israel and Palestine. In the Israeli-Palestinian conflict, Christians are not called to take Israel's side—Christians are called to imitate Israel's Messiah—the Messiah who prioritized reconciliation, taught enemy-love, and gave the world the radical idea of forgiving seventy times seven. The way of Jesus is the alternative way, where justice does not come by suicide bombs or predator drones. This is the way we are called to bear witness to. This alone is the justice that can heal the world. This is justice that Amos longed to roll like a mighty river (Amos 5:24). This is not justice that is blind and holding a sword; this is justice that looks on with love and offers a healing hand.

[Q]

How would it be possible for those involved in the Israeli-Palestinian conflict to offer a healing hand to those in conflict against them? What difference do you believe it could make in the conflict?

The author states, "If God's goal of justice is reconciliation, and the cross is the place where God accomplishes his ultimate justice, then our concept of justice may need reworking." As your group concludes today, think back over all the different situations of injustice you've talked about or thought about this week.

[Q]

In what situations discussed could your group find ways to activate forgiveness and reconciliation?

[Q]

Which situations were so filled with revenge and hate that only God would know how to bring reconciliation?

WRAP UP

The cross of Christ is not the triumph of justice—Calvary was the scene of the ultimate injustice! The cross of Christ is the triumph of forgiveness. The cross is where ultimate injustice encounters ultimate forgiveness in the words, "Father, forgive them." The cross is where we do *not* get what we deserve. The cross is where judgment is passed over in favor of forgiveness so that the whole world might be reconciled. The cross is where justice is reinterpreted by mercy in order to be redefined as reconciliation. This alone is what God calls justice. This is where mercy and truth meet, where justice and peace kiss. The cross is the place where "mercy triumphs over judgment" (James 2:13). Good Friday was the day when mercy triumphed over judgment, because the Son of God abandoned his right to justice and instead asked the Father to forgive.

In your journaling this week, write down some of the times in your life when God's mercy triumphed over judgment. Describe how the mercy of God made you feel in that situation.

LIVING WORD

Therefore, if anyone is in Christ, he is a new creation. The old has passed away; behold, the new has come. All this is from God, who through Christ reconciled us to himself and gave us the ministry of reconciliation.

—2 Corinthians 5:17-18

PRAYER REQUESTS

NOTES

NOTES

{ We have taken a crowbar to the Golden Rule and the narrow gate and tried to pry them apart as if they had nothing to do with one another. This is scandalous! }

THE GOLDEN RULE AND THE NARROW GATE

READ

Read chapter 8 from *Unconditional?* before you meet with the group this week.

BRIAN ZAHND BEGAN chapter 8 with strong words about the Sermon on the Mount: "The significance of the Sermon on the Mount cannot be over-emphasized. The Sermon on the Mount is as important to understanding Jesus as the 'Ninety-Five Theses' is to understanding Martin Luther or the 'I Have a Dream' speech is to understanding Martin Luther King Jr. We cannot imagine trying to understand Luther apart from his 'Ninety-Five Theses' or trying to understand Dr. King apart from his 'I Have a Dream' speech. Likewise it is impossible to understand Jesus apart from his Sermon on the Mount. But here is the scandal: evangelical Christianity has tried to do just that—has tried to understand Jesus apart from the Sermon on the Mount!"

REFLECT

**Take time to consider each of the questions in this section before
you meet with your group, and be prepared to share your answers.**

There is a reason why we avoid the Sermon on the Mount. We are afraid
of it. Its commands are daunting, and its implications are enormous. Any
serious attempt to actually *live* the Sermon on the Mount would require a
profound reevaluation of lifestyles and allegiances. And so we look for a
way out. We employ theologians to tell us how it doesn't mean what it obvi-
ously means. We look for a way to tame the commands of Christ. A way to
domesticate the Sermon on the Mount. A way to painlessly accommodate
the sermon to the status quo. We try to marginalize the Sermon on the
Mount. We attempt to make the radical red letters of Matthew chapters 5, 6,
and 7 largely irrelevant to a very narrow definition of salvation. Here is how
we appeal to the theologians to "save" us from the Sermon on the Mount:
it's done by reducing salvation. ("Honey, I shrunk the gospel.") Once we
have reduced salvation and the purpose of Christ's coming to "how to get to
heaven when you die," the Sermon on the Mount then seems marginal.

[Q]

As you prepare for this week's group meeting, read the fifth, sixth, and
seventh chapters of Matthew. In the space below, briefly describe the major
teachings of Christ in his Sermon on the Mount.

[Q]

Zahnd states, "Once we have reduced salvation and the purpose of Christ's coming to 'how to get to heaven when you die,' the Sermon on the Mount then seems marginal. And it must be marginalized, because if we're not outright afraid of the Sermon on the Mount, we still run into the problem of how it doesn't fit neatly into our evangelical 'system' of salvation." Look more closely at Matthew 5–7. For each of the Scripture references below, write down what Christ is saying that goes beyond the "how to get to heaven when you die" way of looking at salvation.

Matthew 5:13–14

Matthew 5:38–42

Matthew 6:16–18

Matthew 6:24

Matthew 7:1–6

Matthew 7:24–29

As you read chapter 8 this week, carefully consider the quote from Athanasius, a fourth-century bishop in the Greek Orthodox Church. Athanasius reminds us that God created humanity to bear his image, but the image of God in humanity has been stained and marred through sin. Yet God does not *throw away the panel*. God does not abandon his intention for humanity to bear his image. Instead the *subject* sits again so that the image might be repainted. This is the accomplishment of the Incarnation. And it's as we look at Jesus Christ that we remember what we are to look like, what we are to *be* like. Jesus Christ is a human as God intended. Jesus Christ is the one who faithfully bears the image of God and informs us how we should be.

This is why what Jesus is doing in the Sermon on the Mount is so vitally important. Jesus is teaching us and presenting us with the recovered image of God in humanity. Jesus is showing us how to be like God and how to bear God's image. And as we listen to the Sermon on the Mount, the recurring theme is forgiveness. *Blessed are the merciful. Turn the other cheek. Go the second mile. Give your cloak too. Love your enemies. Forgive as you are forgiven.*

[Q]

After reading these two paragraphs, go back and review your answers to each of the Scripture quotes from Matthew 5–7. How are you actively demonstrating the image of Christ in your life as Christ taught in each instance?

DISCUSS

When your small group is meeting to discuss this chapter, focus on discussing the following questions or statements.

In Matthew 7:12–14 Christ sets forth the Golden Rule and the narrow gate. The Golden Rule is the command to treat others on the basis of how we want to be treated. The narrow gate is the difficult way that leads to life. Jesus is saying, "Look, here is the summary of my sermon: treat others on the basis of how you want to be treated. Don't retaliate; forgive. This is the narrow gate. It's hard to do, but it's the road that leads to life." But we have not heard it that way. We've not taught it that way. We have taken a crowbar of horrendously poor biblical interpretation and tried to pry apart the Golden Rule and the narrow gate. Jesus is talking about how to live...*here and now!* Jesus is talking about a way of conduct that leads to life. Jesus is talking about an alternative way, which, though difficult, leads to life—the way of life that won't destroy us.

[Q]

Take time as a group to list some ways that we can treat others on the basis of how we want to be treated.

[Q]

Now list some ways where someone has not been treated in the same way you would want to be treated in that situation.

The author tells us that "Jesus teaches us that the way that seems right, the way that is easy, the popular way, the way in which we are scripted from birth, the way that most people go, is the *wrong* way." The way that seems right is the way that is so pervasive, so popular, so assumed, so scripted by our culture, so endorsed by society that it seems to be the only way available. It is the way of the self-centered agenda. It is the way of getting ahead in life. It's the way of *looking out for number one*. This is the six-lane interstate highway of contemporary culture, which is presented to us in ten thousand commercials. *Drink our beer, drive our car, wear our watch, use our broker—and you'll be sexy, wealthy, cool, and happy!* As we travel the highway of consumerism, the signs all say we're on the road to happiness. But Jesus says the signs are a lie. Jesus says the bridge is out, and the way of self-seeking is the long road to ruin.

[Q]

Our culture today has become so self-absorbed, so self-centered, that it is nearly impossible to see the Golden Rule at work. But it's very easy to see symptoms of our self-centered living. Discuss these symptoms. How do these symptoms keep us from obeying the Golden Rule?

Chapter 8 unveils the link between the Golden Rule and the narrow gate with these words: "Instead of butchering the Sermon on the Mount by severing the Golden Rule from the narrow gate, let's do justice to what Jesus is teaching and see how the two go together—let's learn how to walk the narrow way by learning to live the Golden Rule." The "way" is narrow because living the Golden Rule is hard!

Jesus says, "Look, here is the summary of my sermon: treat others on the basis of how you want to be treated. Don't retaliate; forgive. This is the narrow gate. It's hard to do, but it's the road that leads to life." Jesus is talking about how to live...here and now.

[Q]

How does living the Golden Rule lead to life?

The Beatitudes are the counterintuitive announcements with which Jesus began his Sermon on the Mount. "Part of what the Beatitudes accomplish is to undermine the whole system of basing happiness on lust and pride—the mad pursuit of money, sex, and power. The Beatitudes challenge the basic value system of the fallen world order. As such the principalities and powers will always view the Beatitudes as a subversive threat to their rule—because they are!"

[Q]

How does each beatitude invert the assumptions of our culture?

Blessed are the poor in spirit, for theirs is the kingdom of heaven.

Blessed are those who mourn, for they shall be comforted.

Blessed are the meek, for they shall inherit the earth.

Blessed are those who hunger and thirst for righteousness, for they shall be satisfied.

Blessed are the merciful, for they shall receive mercy.

Blessed are the pure in heart, for they shall see God.

Blessed are the peacemakers, for they shall be called sons of God.

Blessed are those who are persecuted for righteousness' sake, for theirs is the kingdom of heaven.

Blessed are you when others revile you and persecute you and utter all kinds of evil against you falsely on my account.

[Q]

It's important to note that the Golden Rule does not say, "Whatever you wish that *your closest friends* would do to you, do also to them." It says, "Whatever you wish that others would do to you, do also to them." In order to obey what Jesus is teaching us, we must be willing to actively think and imagine what it would be like to be in the place of the other—to be them. This is especially true when the *them* we are called to relate to occupy the role of enemy. Brian Zahnd states, "What would it be like to be an atheist, a radical secularist, gay, Muslim? How would we like to be treated by the Christian community?" It will be impossible to live out the Golden Rule if we are demonizing and dehumanizing *them*. But that is exactly what happens in many instances. Look at each of the following groups and discuss how each should be treated by those who are following the Golden Rule.

Atheist

Radical secularist

Homosexual

Muslim

Sex offender

Serial killer

Abusive spouse

Political opponent

WRAP UP

We live in a world where much is wrong. And what is most wrong with the world is not the politics or the economy or who happens to be living in the White House. What is most wrong with the world is the human heart. The greed and pride and lust of the human heart are the epicenter of all that is wrong with the world. We should realize this by now. As followers of Christ, we are not so much called to know the answer or preach the answer as much as we are called to *be* the answer. This is how we are salt and light (also found in the Sermon on the Mount). We are to model the answer by being Christlike in a Caesar-like world. This is what the Sermon on the Mount is all about.

During the next week, think about your own life. How are you demonstrating the Golden Rule in action? What actions do you need to take to live out the Beatitudes? What actions have you taken that do not exemplify your walk on the narrow way? Journal your answers in the space below.

LIVING WORD

Blessed are the poor in spirit, for theirs is the kingdom of heaven.

Blessed are those who mourn, for they shall be comforted.

Blessed are the meek, for they shall inherit the earth.

Blessed are those who hunger and thirst for righteousness, for they shall be satisfied.

Blessed are the merciful, for they shall receive mercy.

Blessed are the pure in heart, for they shall see God.

Blessed are the peacemakers, for they shall be called sons of God.

Blessed are those who are persecuted for righteousness' sake, for theirs is the kingdom of heaven.

Blessed are you when others revile you and persecute you and utter all kinds of evil against you falsely on my account.

Rejoice and be glad, for your reward is great in heaven.

—Matthew 5:3-12

PRAYER REQUESTS

NOTES

NOTES

{ The hope for peace that I see is where the disciples of Jesus don't just watch in admiration as Jesus carries his cross but practice an imitation of the same kind of cross-bearing forgiveness. }

Session 6

THE PRINCE OF PEACE

READ

Read chapter 10 from *Unconditional?* before you meet with the group this week.

PEACE. PEACE AMONG nations. World peace. It's the wish of dippy beauty queens. It's also the dream of the prophets. In our war-torn world, it's easy to be cynical about any prospects for peace that go beyond the realm of our own private emotions. But the Bible does not endorse such cynicism. In one sense, peace has always been an impossible dream—but a dream the prophets dared to imagine anyway. The first mention of peace among the prophets is when the prophet Isaiah speaks of a Prince of Peace.

> For unto us a child is born,
>   to us a son is given;
> and the government shall be upon his shoulder,
>   and his name shall be called
> Wonderful Counselor, Mighty God,
>   Everlasting Father, Prince of Peace.
> Of the increase of his government and of peace
>   there will be no end.
>
> —ISAIAH 9:6–7

REFLECT

Take time to consider each of the questions in this section before you meet with your group, and be prepared to share your answers.

[Q]

During a time when the nation of Israel lived in the shadow of the ominous Assyrian Empire, the prophet Isaiah envisioned God's deliverance in the form of a child yet to be born—a child who would become a king and bear the responsibility of governance upon his shoulders and succeed where the rest had failed. He speaks of this child in the most superlative ways. The prophesied Son of David will give us wonderful counsel; he will be mighty God among us; he will be the progenitor of a new way of being human; he will be the Prince of Peace. The Bible is filled with demonstrations of God's application of peace upon people and upon situations. In preparation for a discussion of godly peace with your group, look up each of the following Scripture references and write down how God brought peace in each instance.

Psalm 37:37

Psalm 147:14

Isaiah 26:3

Jeremiah 29:11

Luke 1:79

John 16:33

The followers of Christ, who are both the recipients and practitioners of radical forgiveness, should be the leading authorities on peace. Of course, we have to actually practice peace before we can be respected as authorities on the subject. But this is what we are called to in Christ. This is how we are to be the light of the world and the sons of God—through a proclamation and practice of a gospel of peace based in forgiveness.

[Q]

Think about your own life as a follower of Christ. How have you practiced peace in your day-to-day life experiences?

DISCUSS

When your small group is meeting to discuss this chapter, focus on discussing the following questions or statements.

The author says that although the peace of Christ includes personal, inner peace, we must not so privatize the gospel as to make peace only a matter of private mental health. As the apostle Paul writes about the accomplishments of Christ concerning peace in his letter to the Ephesians, his primary emphasis is *not* a private inner peace but a peace between ethnic groups who have had a long history of bitter enmity. In our current global climate, we are seeing an absence of anything that even remotely resembles the peace of Christ. Discuss the various things that are keeping the peace of Christ from being experienced by the nations of our world.

[Q]

What can believers do—in a large *or* small way—to bring peace to a world at war?

Forgiveness has a horizontal dimension as well. This is why in the Lord's Prayer we ask God to forgive us, while in the same breath pledging to forgive others. Forgiveness is God's way of achieving peace. In fact, it is ultimately the only way of achieving peace between alienated parties. Christians should have much to contribute to the subject of peace. In a world bereft of peace and drunk on hostility, Christians are called to be salt and light through the consistent practice of forgiveness-based peace.

[Q]

How can the followers of Christ practice forgiveness-based peace?

[Q]

If the followers of Christ are to be the light of the world through the proclamation and practice of a gospel of peace based in forgiveness, what actions must we take to do this?

Chapter 10 of *Unconditional?* describes Jesus as "the Prince of Peace whose crown was made of thorns, whose throne was a cross, whose acclamation was a mockery, whose triumph was a crucifixion, and whose kingdom was won by shedding his own blood." We discover that only by taking up our own cross and following him—which means nothing less than following his way of doing things—can we be effective at showing God's peace in our world.

As a group, discuss what "taking up your cross" has meant for various people in your group.

[Q]

How did doing this achieve peace in the situation?

[Q]

Discuss the story told in chapter 10 of Brian Zahnd's ride on a train in Paris. How did Zahnd bring forgiveness-based peace to Yu, the young man he met on the train? How did he encourage the young man in his hope for peace? What similar experiences have you had in introducing forgiveness-based peace to those you meet?

The author said that the kingdom of God does not come by political machinations or by military might. It doesn't come by bullets or ballots, by elections or intrigues, by democracies or demagogueries. The kingdom of God comes quietly, almost secretly. It comes through the gradual transformation of hearts and minds one life at a time. The kingdom of God comes in a million different ways as people become fascinated with Jesus Christ, find his forgiveness, and learn to extend it to others. Where is this kingdom? Jesus said it is *among* you. This kingdom is seen and experienced among those who take seriously the call to forgive as we are forgiven, to forgive the sins of others, to forgive the sins of enemies, to forgive unconditionally. This is the kingdom of God. It is radical—and it is the greatest thing ever!

Zahnd gave several examples where he has observed the kingdom of God played out in the life experiences of God's people, examples of followers of Christ extending radical forgiveness that ushers in the peace of God and the kingdom of God.

[Q]

Where have you observed the kingdom of God in the lives of God's people? What suggestions can you give for ways to extend his kingdom in *your* lives, through *your* willingness to forgive unconditionally?

WRAP UP

As followers of the Lamb, we must come to realize that it is only through the practice of radical forgiveness that we can achieve real peace. Peace with God comes by forgiving and being forgiven. We both receive forgiveness and extend forgiveness by faith. Forgiveness is nothing less than faith expressing itself through love (Gal. 5:6). So as the people of faith, we keep on praying day by day, "Forgive us our debts as we forgive our debtors." We keep on forgiving seventy times seven. We keep on forgiving the sins of others and using the keys of the kingdom of heaven to liberate our world from the chains of hatred, which bind us to the cycle of revenge. This is how we follow our crucified and risen Lord. This is how peace comes to our heart, our home, our world. And peace doesn't come any other way. Indeed, no peace is peace but that which comes through the forgiveness of sins.

LIVING WORD

Jesus said to them again, "Peace be with you. As the Father has sent me, even so I am sending you." And when he had said this, he breathed on them and said to them, "Receive the Holy Spirit. If you forgive the sins of anyone, they are forgiven them; if you withhold forgiveness from anyone, it is withheld."

—John 20:21-23

PRAYER REQUESTS

NOTES

NOTES

NOTES